Resonate

Mike,

Praying for you, brother.
You got this. The world
needs your gifts.
    GOD BLESS,
    Sean Stahlkerm

Resonate

Reach Your Peak: Principles of Peak Performance

Sean K. Shahkarami

Published by Game Changer Publishing

Paperback ISBN: 978-1-961189-74-4
Hardcover ISBN: 978-1-961189-75-1
Digital: ISBN: 978-1-961189-76-8

www.GameChangerPublishing.com

Read This First

Just to say thanks for buying and reading my book, I would like to give you a free welcome call with me, no strings attached!

Click this link:

https://calendly.com/seankshahkarami/30min

DEDICATIONS AND GRATITUDES

To Reggie – *May the cream always rise to the top.*

To my daughter, Sadie – *You are my greatest gift and the light in my life. I love you.*

To my wife, Sarah – *Thank you for always supporting me, even when we can't see the vision, we always walk by faith.*

To my publisher – *Thank you for supporting, helping, and encouraging me along this journey.*

To my family – *Thank you for your unconditional love and support.*

To the reader – *Thank you for picking up this book and supporting me. I hope you get everything you're looking for from it, and I wish you the greatest success in all that you do.*

Resonate

Reach Your Peak: Principles of Peak Performance

Sean K. Shahkarami

www.GameChangerPublishing.com

Table of Contents

Introduction

As far back as I can remember, I've always had a passion for reading. I recall staying up way past my bedtime in elementary school to read Harry Potter under the covers with a flashlight. In high school, I was fortunate to have an exceptional English teacher who helped me excel in writing literature essays. In his class, I discovered my love of American literature when we first read *The Great Gatsby*. Shortly after, I stumbled upon my favorite book and author, *East of Eden* by John Steinbeck, the most significant piece of literary art I've ever read. At that point, I knew I wanted to be a published author someday. However, I was aware that becoming a published author would be a long and arduous process. I was fortunate to have practical parents and teachers who instilled a sense of pragmatism and balanced my idealism.

Despite my desire to be a published author, I had no formal training in writing outside of high school. I did not have an English degree and never took a creative writing class. But I also knew that if I were to write anything of value, it would take years of practice, refinement, and mastery. I began working on my craft during my junior year of high school, writing poetry and short stories, and continued to practice throughout college. I also kept my love of reading, eventually transitioning from fiction to self-improvement, self-discovery, and neuroscience.

I am a CPA with a Bachelor's in Business Administration and a Master's in Accounting. I am the founder and owner of two businesses, Opilio and

Resonate. Opilio (Latin for "shepherd," in case you were wondering) is an AI and machine learning automation business that focuses on automating complex processes, providing real-time business intelligence, and predicting future outcomes. Resonate is a coaching service that helps individuals, influencers, athletes, and entrepreneurs perform at their peak and is based on the principles in this book.

Formerly, I held a director-level position at one of the largest accounting and consulting firms globally, where I helped lead the healthcare and life sciences M&A (mergers and acquisitions) consulting group. I have more than ten years of M&A experience and nine specific to the healthcare industry. I was raised blue-collar, the son of an immigrant father who instilled in me a strong work ethic, and a mother who taught me the importance of generosity and service.

I decided to write this book now because I sense its urgency and need. The COVID lockdowns and the proliferation of artificial intelligence and machine learning are disrupting and will disrupt every industry over the next three years. What we believe to be true today will be challenged and upended at a rate faster than anyone has ever witnessed before in recorded human history. As your friend and mentor, I wrote this book aimed at those in professional careers, students, entrepreneurs, athletes, and anyone searching for a life with deep meaning and purpose. Based on my synthesis of renowned authors and leaders, my philosophy takes a holistic approach that will help not just in your career but in all aspects of your life.

This book will cover abstract ideas, concepts, and theories balanced with real-world examples from my experiences. It will provide practical tools and applications to help you ritualize the content in real life. These exercises and practices will be challenging but worth your time, commitment, and total effort. Remember, knowledge by itself will not help you. The training and application of knowledge lead to fundamental behavioral changes and rewire your brain chemistry and neural pathways. Developing these skills will set you apart and equip you to resonate along your journey to realizing your goals and unique purpose in life. Thank you for joining me on this journey.

CHAPTER 1

The Best is Yet to Come

It's interesting because where I'm going to start this book is towards the end of my 10-year journey in self-improvement and learning peak performance principles, how to apply them, how they can transform your life, the importance of developing the mindset of a champion, and how to be the best version of yourself in all aspects of life.

Strangely enough, sport, not business, led me to the most recent breakthroughs. See, I took up golf about four years ago and instantly fell in love. The first couple of years were very challenging, and much of my practice time was spent learning the fundamentals and technical skills of the golf swing. Starting at about a 24-handicap, I was able to cut it in half with two years of grit and old-fashioned work ethic. I told my coach that I wanted to keep going with the goal of winning the club championship one day, which would require becoming a scratch golfer even to contend.

At this point, my coach told me the difference between my golf game and a scratch golfer was the six inches between my ears. Many know golf is a mental game, and much of your success will depend on your mental state. As someone who's always been successful through hard work and grit, learning fundamentals, and running drills, I didn't know where to start from a mental game perspective. My coach was helpful, but he, too, is very much focused on the technical and fundamental skills of the golf swing and game. So being a natural reader, that's where I started with books.

I discovered two books written by Jayne Storey, *Connected Golf* and *Breathe Golf*. What's most interesting is the author's story; she is not a golfer. She studied Eastern philosophy in China and studied martial arts for most of her career. She became interested in the game of golf after reading an interview with Jack Nicklaus when she heard Nicklaus say that the golf swing starts with the feet. She related it back to her training in Tai chi and started discovering the similarities between her training in ancient martial arts and the golf swing.

Essentially, one of the main ideas I got from that book was that the golf swing should feel effortless. It might sound like a paradox, but when you watch the pros play, their game does look effortless. In fact, watching almost any professional sport, the game itself appears effortless to the players playing the game. Moreover, applying the principles I learned from her books, I instantly started playing better golf.

It really should not be as big of a surprise as it was, I mean, if you watch sports at all and you see an elite player like Tom Brady, Michael Jordan, Kobe Bryant, Muhammad Ali, Mike Trout, Clayton Kershaw, etc., you will see those guys are locked in and the way they move around their respective field or court, it looks as if they aren't even trying. Storey would likely say they are playing the game in a meditative state. I naturally began questioning my own experiences – if this is true in professional sports, hell, if an amateur golfer sees a two to three-stroke improvement almost instantly from nothing more than breathwork, relaxation, and mental reconditioning, shouldn't this also be true in other professional careers?

Could the lessons be applied to my job? Could I actually be more productive while also being more balanced? Could I accomplish more with less effort? I do not believe the timing of this was coincidental, either. At the time, I had recently been promoted to Director. I was 32 years old, with a family and a growing list of obligations and commitments. I became extremely overwhelmed. The practice was still running hot, and I was leading thirteen different projects at one point. I wasn't sleeping well, and I started dealing with something I had never struggled with ever before. I couldn't focus.

Back then, I had no idea why. I just knew that my entire life, I had always differentiated myself not by being the smartest or the most talented, but by my ability to pay close attention to complex tasks and seeing them through to completion. It got so bad I would walk into a room for a specific reason, and once there, I had forgotten why I walked into the room. I contemplated seeing a doctor for ADHD or even potentially something more serious.

The only reason I did not end up going to a doctor was because I did not want to solve my problem with pills unless it became an absolute last resort. I wanted to take a holistic approach if I could. I started doing all the online research I could to figure out what was going on. How could I control the stressors in high-pressure situations, find focus, and still be able to perform at a high level?

Maybe the most distressing aspect of this crisis was it happened only about a year ago. I had already been through so much adversity (we will circle back to this) and employed several techniques, strategies, and practices to cope with stress. I prioritized my physical body's health and fitness and guarded my mind to keep it sharp. I thought I had already created a strong system that would have prevented something like this from happening.

Fortunately, through my research, I found some answers and some mind-blowing statistics…

Did you know?

- In an eight-hour day, the average knowledge worker typically only has anywhere from 45 to 60 minutes of productive work.

- On average, of those 45 to 60 minutes, only 11 minutes are spent fully focused.

Now, maybe if you work in Corporate America, you are not too surprised. Let's be honest if your work looks anything like how mine used to, you know much of our day is spent on low-value meetings, especially the ones without an agenda that never end (and yes, I have been on not just one, but two calls that went over eight hours), constant emails, teams or Slack instant messages. Then when you start adding in the self-distractions most of us are now conditioned to engage in, like mindlessly browsing the internet, scrolling Facebook, Instagram, TikTok, Twitter (I heard Meta is about to drop Threads now, too), and the list goes on and on of the endless ways to get instant dopamine hits (similar to drugs).

Many of you may have seen *The Social Dilemma*, a Netflix documentary detailing the dark side of social media. Here's the thing, while all of that is true – it's not just social media. It's literally just about everything – everything is fighting for your attention, wanting your focus. It is up to us to choose, and wisely I may add, what we put our focus on. It just gets exacerbated online because technology has evolved exponentially to the point we no longer know what a healthy relationship with technology looks or feels like. Maybe not all, but some of you, if you are near my age or older, do you remember the time in your childhood when the iPhone did not exist? When the internet was some weird noises over a home phone line connection, which came every couple of months in the mail from an AOL CD-ROM disc?

Here's the point, that was when technology was a tool we used when we needed to use it. It did not own us. We owned it. You see, through my research, I found and joined a group called the *Flow Research Collective (FRC)*, which was started by Steve Kotler, one of the leaders in the neuroscience behind flow and peak performance.

I found the reason for my deteriorating mental awareness was not that I had lost my focus. I never got to truly focus because I would get interrupted by the minute-by-minute deluge of corporate communications. Learning from the FRC, I found out the answer is yes – it is possible to be more productive with less effort, and I was able to build habits that helped me reduce those distractions and build my system. It's actually really simple but not exactly easy. It takes commitment to breaking a lot of bad habits we have grown accustomed to, dopamine addictions, and even thinking differently about how we may have been trained to work – sneak preview – despite what any of your bosses may tell you, it is a scientific fact that it is not good for you or conducive for long-term productivity to be constantly connected to your email or work phone. Moreover, I quickly realized the principles upon which the Flow Research Collective was based weren't anything new.

In fact, my system, and most systems out there, are founded on principles that have been around for thousands of years. Plato, Aristotle, and Socrates all spoke of similar principles in life. The Stoics, such as Seneca or Marcus Aurelius, spoke about them. If you go into the Bible, King Solomon in Proverbs and Ecclesiastes, and Jesus Christ, the Messiah, spoke of these principles.

Here are just a few of my favorite quotes as examples of what I mean:

- *"Human behavior flows from three main sources: desire, emotion, and knowledge."* – Plato

- *"I'm trying to think, don't confuse me with facts."* – Plato

- *"He is richest who is content with the least, for content is the wealth of nature."* – Socrates

- *"True wisdom comes to each of us when we realize how little we understand about life, ourselves, and the world around us."* – Socrates

- *"Good habits formed at youth make all the difference."* – Aristotle

- *"True happiness is to enjoy the present, without anxious dependence upon the future, not to amuse ourselves with either hopes or fears but to rest satisfied with what we have, which is sufficient, for he that is so wants nothing. The greatest blessings of mankind are within us and within our reach. A wise man is content with his lot, whatever it may be, without wishing for what he has not."* – Seneca

- *"The happiness of your life depends on the quality of your thoughts."* – Marcus Aurelius

- *"You have power over your mind – not outside events. Realize this, and you will find strength."* – Marcus Aurelius

- *"Call out for insight, and cry aloud for understanding."* – Proverbs 2:3

- *"To learn the truth, you must long to be teachable, or you can despise correction and remain ignorant."* – Proverbs 12:1

- *"What has been will be again, what has been done will be done again; there is nothing new under the sun."* – Ecclesiastes 1:9

- *"But seek first his kingdom and his righteousness, and all these things will be given to you as well. Therefore do not worry about tomorrow, for tomorrow will worry about itself. Each day has enough trouble of its own."* – Matthew 6:33-34

Perhaps, from the quotes, you are starting to sense the same idea I get when I study these principles, which have stood the test of time. I've started to realize that life itself is an endless paradox. The harder we cling, the tighter we squeeze, the faster we lose something. The more we want, the more we covet, the less we seem to have.

Ultimately, one story that really stuck with me was something that Tony Robbins spoke about that happened during his journey and led to who he is today. He said he was constantly asking himself questions. *Why does this happen to me? Why am I not successful? Why does this always seem to happen to me?* I know I have asked myself those same questions, and I'm sure you have too.

Well, one day, he realized maybe he needed to ask better questions. Rather than asking, *Why did this happen to me?* or *Why am I not successful?* He started to reframe his questions. He began asking himself, *What can I learn from this situation? How can I become successful?* Earlier, we touched on where our brains are limited and have not kept up with the growth of technology. While that may be true, the human brain is still the most powerful supercomputer on the planet, and it is really good at answering questions. So when you ask yourself why you aren't successful, you better believe your mind will come up with a million reasons why you aren't.

Maybe this has happened to you – I know it's happened to me:

"You're not successful because you are full of dumb ideas."

"You're not successful because you aren't tall enough."

And these are just lighter answers; for some, you may have trained your brain to be a terrifying, cruel, and self-loathing critic. You can see that if you ask your brain questions that prompt negative answers, your subconscious will continue the same cycle you've been stuck in perpetuity if you let it.

But if you change your questions, you can powerfully change your life. I know this is true because I did it for myself. Through ten years of my own research, accelerated over the past 12 months, I developed my own system of principles. I call the system **Resonate**. Resonate really is the perfect word because the definition itself means to carry or have importance or significance with someone or something, meaning that resonance is not independent. It is dependent. It takes more than one person or thing to resonate truly. One of the most powerful manifestations of resonance is in music, which holds a special place for me as it's a medium of art that has helped me get through challenging times in my own life.

I also love the word because the RESONATE system is also an acronym, and each letter symbolizes a principle. Principles aren't rules, they are guides that give my system flexibility and make it dynamic. What works for me may not work for you, and that's okay. I'll share what works for me, but it will ultimately be up to you to find what works for you. The principles, however, remain the same.

Rhythm

Emotion

Sequence

Order

Nature

Attitude

Training

Excellence

As these principles become more clearly defined, you will see that the principles are designed to keep us grounded in the present moment, with a vision, faith, and hope for the future – knowing that no matter the challenges we may be facing at any given time that they will pass and the best is yet to come.

CHAPTER 2

Purpose

It was a Saturday in September of 2013. It was warm, sunny, and beautiful weather. I woke up late, which was no surprise. I had just spent three nights in the office, getting maybe an hour of sleep underneath my desk, speeding home while guzzling down whatever energy drink was trendy at the time—probably a Red Bull. I would shower, change into a new pair of dress slacks, dress shirt, and tie, and I'd speed back to work as quickly as I possibly could to make sure I wasn't a minute past 7 a.m.

To some, it might sound like a nightmare, but at that moment, it wasn't to me. No, at that moment, I'd reached the pinnacle. Despite attending a non-target university, I was one of 30 out of 3,000 applications to receive and accept a full-time position as an investment banking analyst. And though it wasn't at a bulge bracket bank, it was not a boutique bank either. It was a national bank that had a strong reputation, a storied history and had taken two current Fortune 100 companies public. I was on top of the world. In my own eyes, I'd already made it (whatever "it" means or even is, and well on my way to becoming an arrogant, cocky son of a bitch, I'm sure).

I remember that it was a Saturday because I was the groomsman in one of my best friend's weddings. At that time, in the investment banking industry, analysts did not have weekends off. It was a grueling seven-day work week, but

I'd gotten approval to attend the wedding because it had been planned before my start date, and I'd committed to working overtime (I use overtime loosely as I lack a better term, but how is overtime even possible when you're already working between 90 and 110 hours a week; I still don't have an answer for that question) the days leading up to the wedding, hence the three all-nighters in a row.

I remember waking up feeling hazy. Fortunately, I'd just gotten an espresso machine, as I was basically living off of caffeine and energy drinks at the time. I gulped down three full shots of Espresso, grabbed my things, and jumped in my car, headed to the Chapel. It wasn't a terribly far drive, but it was across town, and I was still a little bit unfamiliar with where I lived as I had really only driven to and from work. The interstates were under construction, and I ended up taking the wrong exit. It was looking more and more like I was going to be late. Unacceptable, I thought. I'm never late. As the GPS was rerouting, I hit the gas.

Damn, the GPS was taking forever, I remember thinking. Finally, it updated with the new route. My exit was only a half mile away. Perfect. I was already in the right-hand lane, and somehow, I was still going to make it on time. It wasn't until I started taking the exit that I realized I was going way too fast, and by then, it was way too late.

I lost control of the car. I swerved to miss a wall. Suddenly, I was airborne, the car flipping over the retaining wall and rolling down a grassy hill on the side of the freeway. My only vivid memory from that moment is when I was upside down, midair—a single moment that felt like a lifetime. I'm not sure if my whole life flashed before my eyes, but I do remember having a reel of visions. I thought, *This is it. All my hard work, all of my achievements, all of the sacrifices, everything about my life, cut off prematurely, everything wasted in vain. This is how I die.* I saw a vision of my parents, a vision of my own obituary in the local newspaper. *This is what I'll be remembered for,* I thought.

Then my mind started to race. *When was the last time I prayed, read the Bible, been to Church?* No answer. In those final moments, I remember I just started praying for forgiveness, praying that my parents, sister, and friends would be okay. And most of all, I prayed that even though I was undeserving, I wanted to go to heaven. I didn't even pray to survive, not because I didn't want to, but because there was no way I was going to survive. I knew what was coming next over the wall. I was about to drop anywhere from 10 to 20 feet and roll down a hill. I closed my eyes and let go of the steering wheel. And as best I could, I surrendered to the coming imminent death.

And then the car stopped rolling. I opened my eyes; it felt like I was in a dream. Somehow, someway, I was alive. Not only alive, but there was no pain. If you know me, you know that I faint at the sight of blood, so I was scared to look down. But I knew I needed to check myself out. Slowly, I looked down at my body—no blood, no broken bones, and I could move my arms, legs, and head. Wow. One problem: my cell phone had ejected through the broken windows of my car. No way to call 911.

The car had stopped on its side, with the driver's side pointing up to the sky. I didn't have a safe way of getting out of the car. The doors were smashed up, and even if they would open, there'd be no way to get out without potentially having the car roll over on me. Fortunately, the sunroof had shattered, and as safely as I could, I unclipped my seat belt and crawled out through the sunroof. A good Samaritan who saw the accident must have called 911 for me because, not long afterward, paramedics and firefighters arrived on the scene.

I don't remember much from our interactions, but I remember the paramedics being amazed and a kind police officer letting me sit in his vehicle and letting me borrow his cell phone so I could call my parents. I'll never forget what he said to me, especially after I declined further medical attention (I still made it to the wedding that day).

He said, "Son, I hope you know how lucky you are. You should have been sent home today. Make sure you realize that."

When my dad arrived, it became an emotional experience. He saw my car before he saw me and thought I was dead. Once he became convinced that I was still alive and realized I was still determined as hell to make it to the wedding, he drove me to the junkyard lot where the car had been towed. Somehow, I was able to fish out my tuxedo from the mangled car.

I remember arriving at the Chapel. When people first saw me, it was like they were looking at a ghost. I didn't realize that I was still caked in dust and broken glass. Thank goodness the bridesmaids took over and started brushing the broken shards of glass off of me, out of my hair, and used baby wipes as a pseudo shower to get the dirt and dust off my hands and face. I did make it to the wedding, but the rest of the day is still a blur to me.

I also found out my memory of the accident is incomplete. I did not lie or embellish my account of the story, but what I did not know and still don't remember is that when I missed my first exit and was taking the second exit, I was not in the right-hand lane. I was in the far-left lane. I crossed three lanes between 90 and 100 miles per hour, trying to make that second exit. That swerve from the far-left lane is why I lost control of my car. They knew because of what was reported on the 911 call. When they looked at the tread marks where my car left the freeway. I'd fallen asleep and didn't even realize it. If you can believe it, I stayed asleep a little while longer. I returned to work the next day (Yep, on Sunday). I shrugged off the car accident as no big deal.

I was tough as nails. Nothing could stop me. Nothing could slow me down. About a week and a half later, I was at my computer, and something *did* slow me down. It was about 9 p.m., which is early in terms of an investment banking work day (9 p.m. to 2 a.m. That's when the real work gets done). I started feeling dizzy. My body started having a sensation I never felt before. It was like the whole world was spinning around me. I started to feel nauseous, and I was sweating. I started to panic. I thought I might be having a heart attack. I asked some coworkers for help, and they decided I should go to the ER. I didn't want to make too big of a deal out of it, so even though I probably should have called an ambulance, I ended up driving myself to the nearby ER, which luckily wasn't far.

They ran tests I don't remember the names of, asked me a lot of questions, and hooked me up to an IV. Finally, the doctor came in. A nice guy. He was tall, thin, and middle-aged. He asked me about my job and the car accident.

Then he said something very similar to the police officer on the day of the accident.

"Son, you may have walked away from that car accident without a scratch, but you did suffer a severe concussion. You're lucky you managed as well as you did until now. Frankly, I'm not sure how you did it. But if you don't want to risk long-term brain damage, you'll have to lie in a dark room. No lights, no TV, no phone, no screens, no music, no reading, no noise, no stimulus for two weeks."

Finally, I started to wake up to the truth. I hadn't told anyone that I'd hit my head in my car accident because I wanted to make it to the wedding so badly. I found out I had had a vertigo attack. I felt fear, real fear. My mind was my greatest asset, and it was threatened. Thankfully, I ended up surrendering to the severity of the situation. I asked for a note to give to my work and promised to do exactly as he said. I went to my parent's house and basically slept for two full weeks.

This may sound crazy, but those two weeks were probably the best thing that I could have ever done. I stayed in that dark room and disconnected from the entire world for two weeks. I was so exhausted from everything. It wasn't boring. It was easy. It was easy just to lie there, rest, think, and sleep. It was almost as if I hit a pause button on my life. It gave me time to reflect and ask myself important questions.

- Is this lifestyle something I can handle?
- Is this what I want out of my life?
- Is this who I am and who I want to become?

Ultimately, I made the decision to give it one last shot at my job. But when I returned, I knew it wasn't going to work. The next day, I turned in my resignation letter. At that time, I thought I was quitting because I thought there would be no way I could ever catch up from missing two weeks. But I realized now that I quit because that job, as prestigious and glamorous as it was, wasn't part of who I am, and it wasn't what I wanted my identity to be tied to anymore. After going through the experiences of almost dying in a car accident, going back to work, and then having a vertigo attack from a severe, undiagnosed concussion (that was due to my pride and not telling people I had hit my head), I felt that there was something more meaningful than just being lucky. I felt as if God had spared me for a bigger reason and a bigger purpose than just this career.

After I turned in my resignation letter, I started wrestling with life's most difficult existential questions—meaning, fulfillment, potential, purpose. *What was my purpose?* I should have died, but I didn't. I'm a walking, breathing miracle. I understand not everyone will have the same beliefs I do, but for me, God was communicating something important. I had a mission that I had not yet accomplished. It was up to me to figure out just what my mission was.

Today, I know what my identity and purpose are. Identity and purpose are the first two building blocks of the fundamentals of my system. I imagine it's the first step of 99% of all the self-help systems out there, too, and there's a reason for that. It's not a cheesy exercise you do to figure out your personality. It is a continuous journey and the only starting point that will ultimately lead to a life of fulfillment. You must know exactly who you are, and you must have a clearly defined purpose.

That's me on the day of the wedding with the groom. Looking back at this, I don't know how I did it.

CHAPTER 3

Man in the Mirror

Initially, after my car accident, there was a time when I felt such a release; a huge weight, and burden off my shoulders. I think it was one of the first times in my life that I felt free since early childhood. I thought things were finally about to get a little bit easier. As I started grappling with who I was, I thought my finding my next career step would be straightforward. After all, I had excellent grades, internships, and hell, though it was short-lived, I had been an investment banker!

I was probably a bit naive, but I remember I started filling out applications. I took it seriously. I know I didn't want to let down my parents. I didn't want to be unemployed for too long. I remember the first couple of weeks, I treated it like a day job. I spent eight hours a day doing applications. Back then, even just ten years ago, job applications were not as easy as they are today. There was no easy application on LinkedIn to get your name in the bucket. Headhunters were not nearly as prevalent, especially not at the entry-level. Each job application probably took an hour to an hour and a half or longer. I'd write eloquent cover letters and have multiple versions or refine my resume for each specific role, highlighting my different experiences.

That process took about a month. I recall receiving just one phone call, and it didn't even result in an in-person interview. I eventually got an in-person interview, but it became evident quickly that the job wasn't a legitimate opportunity. By this point, it was Thanksgiving. I went to my parent's house, and as we sat around the table, my mom and dad asked me how my application process and the job hunt were coming along. I said, "It's been really, really difficult.

At first, my dad said, "Well, you must not be putting in enough time."

"Yeah, I haven't really been able to apply anywhere lately because I've applied to every single job in this area that fits my education and background, and there's nothing left to apply to."

Even my mom, at that point, was frustrated. "You mean you've applied to every job?"

I responded, "Yeah. Here, I'll show you." We walked over to their computer, and I said, "Okay, think of any company, bank, or accounting firm or somewhere you think my background would fit." She typed in a name, pulled it up, and I told her, "Okay, hit the 'apply now' button, and put in my name and email address. Now hit enter." Over and over, the screen would not open the application but say something along the lines of:

"Thank you for your interest. We've already received your application. We will inform you of the next steps, or you may reapply in six months."

We went through five or six of them until my parents said, "Wow, he really has applied to every possible place that we all could think of." At this point, we started thinking if just applying to places outside of my degree made more sense.

I remember it got really dark about that time. I was starting to become really depressed, and I felt like a failure. It was so strange, though, because, on one hand, I knew I had so much to be thankful for, and I was developing in so many ways as a person, but it still seemed as if my worth and value came down to whatever job title and paycheck I held.

I remember lying in bed one day, fighting against the temptation of a victimhood mentality. It was becoming easier and easier to blame other people, other things, for my circumstances. I started thinking to myself, you know what? Yeah, this is a hard time in my life, but I'm young. No matter what happens, it's going to be okay. Me struggling to find a job after what I've been through doesn't make me worthless, and my worth isn't tied to a job. Maybe for the first time ever, I started to really practice gratitude. Instead of thinking about the challenges, I focused on and was grateful for all the awesome things that had taken place during that time.

I had found a new church. I joined a life group there and made new friends in the group. I started thinking, when was the last time you were plugged into a church community? Not since Junior High, I was certain. I had started to go out on a few dates, when before, I didn't have one free second to go out on a date. I began realizing so much of my time spent, even in college, was devoted to academics and whatever extracurriculars would help me get a job in investment banking. I just started thinking about all the things I could do for once that I just didn't have time for in the past because my priorities were so unhealthy and unbalanced.

And that's when I started to discover my identity apart from job titles, achievements, accolades, things. I started to tell myself things like:

- My identity is that I'm a good person.
- I'm a good son.
- I'm a good friend.
- Truly, my identity is in Jesus, and I'm a child of God, and no matter what the world thinks of me, my worth isn't truly found here.

Now, since then, my identity has matured. In fact, my identity is distilled down with brevity and ultimate clarity. I am blessed and unconquerable. Some of the things that helped me distill my identity are some other fundamentals to my system: Release negative emotions and relationships. Replace everything toxic in your life with positive content.

I started listening to a ton of motivational speakers on YouTube. One of the earliest ones I picked up on was Eric Thomas, who has a quote I absolutely love to this day about identity and purpose: "Success is the ability, at any moment, to sacrifice who you are for who you want to become."

More recently, I read a book called, *Be Your Future Self Now* by Dr. Benjamin Hardy. It is full of insight on how to self-actualize who you want to become. Dr. Hardy details that up until the early 1920s, most people in the field of psychology, most doctors, wrote and believed that a person is essentially the culmination of their past. All the choices you've made, all those consequences of your past choices, culminate into who you are at any given moment. While I don't discount the past, I've always felt that rather than looking backward, what if it's actually our future pulling us forward? It was interesting because that's exactly what Dr. Hardy is describing in his book.

One of Dr. Hardy's anecdotal stories that stuck with me was the story of Viktor Frankl (author of *Man's Search for Meaning*). Frankl was a Jewish psychologist and actually one of the pioneers of more forward/future-looking psychology theories while living in Germany as Hitler took power in the country. Ultimately, he was separated from his wife and the rest of his family, ending up in Auschwitz. It's a long story, but essentially, Frankl, by writing his book and putting his theories of keeping faith in a brighter future, helped others cling to hope.

It's almost unimaginable and puts a lot of things into perspective when you think of what some other people have had to endure and what they survived. Keeping this perspective close in mind, practicing gratitude for all the small joys and blessings is the key to developing an unshakeable identity and fighting off the temptation to succumb to a victim mentality.

Lastly, developing this strong sense of self will help you stay true to your core values. As a consistent high achiever, I always carried a lot of responsibility and a lot of commitments, and over the course of the years, I had become somewhat of a "yes-man" and people pleaser. I started to realize I did a lot of things just out of other people's expectations for me and did not necessarily even know what my wants and expectations were for myself.

I think that's when it dawned on me that though I knew and believed my life had been spared for a specific purpose, I wouldn't be able to find that purpose until I truly reconstructed and could define my own identity. I needed to know with clarity and conviction exactly who I was and what values I stood for. If I did not follow through with that commitment to define my identity, then I would just fall into the same cycle of living a life that someone else wanted for me and not what I wanted for myself.

You may think that's a little bit of a bold statement, and I get it; no one holds a gun to our heads (I hope not, at least) and forces us to live life how they see fit, but there are definitely influences to these decisions that creep in, many times innocently, or even well-intentioned if we are not firm in our identities. In fact, did you know the number one regret of a dying person is that they wish they had lived a life true to themselves and not others?

I'll give you a couple of examples. First, I had no idea what investment banking was when I first went to college. I got into a Business Honors program at TCU, and it was just expected that the cream of the crop would try to go to Wall Street and work in investment banking.

Now, before you think that I am about to contradict myself regarding the victimhood mentality, let me clarify. I don't blame the University, but what I am pointing out is everyone, and I mean absolutely everyone, has an agenda.

It's not bad, per se; it's just the truth. For the University, the agenda had the best of intentions. The thought was that we have this incredible honors program, the University has invested heavily in the Business School, which is now a top 30 national program, but we are a non-target school for some of the more prestigious banking jobs. How do we change that? We change that by helping our best students get those jobs despite the challenges. And they did! TCU was an incredible resource – it still is for me today!

There was no ill intent behind their agenda; they were doing the best they could for their students and future students. But see, when I was in college, I didn't have a strong identity. To be brutally honest with my past self – I was completely insecure and tried to cover up my own insecurities by being the smartest and most arrogant person around. When you are that insecure, and you don't have a strong sense of self and strong core values, you'll go in any direction that seems trendy. At that time, the trend was investment banking.

As I started realizing these things about myself, I started realizing the first step to creating a strong identity was to unwrap the identity I currently held. During those formative years, my self-defined identity was always wrapped with some kind of achievement:

- "Sean, the Neeley Fellow."
- "Sean, the investment banker."

Here's the problem. Tying your identity to some *thing* will always set you up for failure and heartbreak because *things* can always be lost, stolen, and taken away. My advice is to build your identity based on feelings and emotions. Ask yourself how you want to feel. How do you want others to feel about you? Answering those questions will lead you in the right direction. The starting point is staring down and getting comfortable with the person looking back at you in the mirror.

It's okay, I think, sometimes to do things to please other people, but it's also very important to know when to say no, and how to say no. I think it's a common problem because as I follow different types of newsletters of people who all speak about self-development, healthy habits, and peak performance, I see time and time again advice on how to say no.

CHAPTER 4

I Won't Back Down

One of the more popular sayings in business is, "It's not what you know, it's who you know." Now, I'm a big believer that true success is two-fold: it is what you know, and it is also who you know. However, during this time of my life, I was just becoming more comfortable being more vulnerable and asking people for help. Up until this point, I was full of pride and arrogance, determined to do everything on my own, so I guess it makes sense how everything played out in my life shortly after that Thanksgiving when I finally surrendered my identity.

I found my next job about a week or two afterward, heading into the Christmas season. I had been using the holidays as a time to reconnect with old friends I hadn't seen. I had a friend and former roommate of mine at TCU. He recently got a job at a smaller firm with a nationally recognized healthcare management consulting group. They were doing well in that division and were making investments to grow in that area of their business.

I remember when I first reached out to Brandon. I think at that time, it was probably the first time I had been that honest, that vulnerable, with someone else outside of my family in my life. I caught him up on what happened to me, and I did, of course, detail all the positive things that were taking place, but I also did not try and embellish how I was doing in my career (or lack thereof).

"You know, despite the silver linings that came from the car accident, which I am grateful for. There is one area I am really struggling with. I have had no luck finding a new job. To be completely honest, I have only gotten maybe one or two callbacks. Not only am I a little bit worried, but I'm also embarrassed."

And then I made the ask.

"If you know anyone hiring, could you let me know, and if possible, be a referral or reference?"

It is such a simple thing, but something I struggled with and have seen many other smart, talented, ambitious people struggle with as well—to ask for help.

As a short aside, asking for help is not a show of weakness. It is a sign of strength and intelligence. It takes wisdom to know when to ask for help. It makes you human and relatable. Asking for help may be one of the most underrated leadership skills. Yes, leadership, the ability to ask for help, is a sign of a great leader. In fact, I ask for help more often now. With more life experience comes more responsibilities and obligations. Furthermore, the more things I learn, the more I am humbled by all the things I do not know. I ask for help in basically everything I do, including writing and coaching. I still get coached and actually have more coaches in my life than ever before!

Brandon got me an interview, and I ended up accepting the job there. I started basically right after New Year's Day in 2014. Those two years at that firm are some of the best years of my career and were the most formative in shaping the expertise I have today.

I wish I could say it was just pure grit, work, and talent because it is the place where I really cut my teeth in healthcare, but I can't take all that credit. What we were doing was highly complex. We were essentially modeling insurance contracts for large hospitals and healthcare organizations, and I mean, we were modeling these complex contracts to the penny. I don't expect everyone to understand what I am talking about, but to put it simply, most of you probably have health insurance. Your insurance company has a contract with the doctor you go see, and that contract stipulates the amount of money the insurance company will pay your doctor when you go in for an appointment. As you may imagine, it is a large amount of data that we had to analyze to quantify the contracts, and back then, we were using Microsoft Access databases. I wouldn't say we had to be experts in SQL coding, but we had to learn enough to be dangerous. I remember opening up the VBA editor and writing in custom code to properly run the queries.

There were several nights when the data sets would be so large in the database that we would run the query and go to bed that night and just pray that when we woke up the next morning, the query had finished with the right results. Otherwise, we'd have to spend the eight-plus hour workday re-running the query and get a loaner laptop to stay busy doing other work. The worst was when the query would time out and not finish!

As you can imagine, it was tedious, demanding, and detailed work. It's not to say that I didn't do well, but there was a part of me I think had a little bit of resistance and overwhelm when I first started trying to learn these skills. It was completely different from what I had been used to, and I had spent a great deal of time becoming proficient in Microsoft Excel. There was definitely a part of me that still saw myself as a banker. I wasn't quite convinced how this Microsoft Access stuff was going to benefit me in my career.

I remember probably a couple of months, maybe a little later after I came on, we ended up hiring another guy. He had graduated from the University of Texas. He also knew Brandon. His name was Reggie. Not that it really matters, other than I want to give you a little bit of context about Reggie, he was black, and we were in Fort Worth, Texas. Now, do not get me wrong, I have been a Fort Worth native my whole life, and it's a great place to grow up and live.

Discrimination and racism are pretty rare, but every once in a while, it will rear its ugly head.

There was one Friday night when we had all gone out together to a few of the local bars, and as we were leaving, another guy started making remarks. I was walking right beside Reggie, and I remember I was about to say something, and Reggie must have read my facial expressions because he put his arm around my shoulder, smiled as only Reggie could smile, and said, "Sean, it's not worth it man, let's keep on walking." I nodded in agreement, kept my mouth shut, and then we heard the word. I turned to Reggie, and again he must have just read my facial expressions because he just continued smiling. He shook his head no and just said, "You think I have never heard that word before? Don't give him the response he wants. Let's all get home safe tonight."

I bring this up because Reggie was also one of those guys who had beaten the odds. He was from the South Dallas/Oak Cliff area, which is not the most affluent neighborhood, to say the least. He got accepted to the University of Texas on a scholarship, and to quote one of Reggie's high school friends, he had used "his brain as his ticket out of the hood." Not only did Reggie manufacture his way out, he had become disciplined not to let anything or anyone threaten his progress. I believe one of the reasons Reggie was able to handle that situation with such grace was that he had already overcome so much adversity in his life that what happened that night was so insignificant to him it wasn't even worth acknowledging.

I remember I learned so much just watching and observing him. He was typically the first person in the door every morning and typically the last to leave. And I remember that was kind of my own M.O. at the time, so we'd often find ourselves walking out of the office together. We'd talk, get to know each other, chat about life on our way out of the building. I remember one evening, we were walking to the parking garage, the cars, and I said, "I thought you didn't have a project. What were you doing so late tonight? You're not staffed on anything. I'll never forget his response because it is something I have adopted and still practice for anything new I am trying to learn.

He replied, "Actually, I was running through old models." He was going through old Access databases, and he said, "I was reverse engineering them so that I could understand how to do it better myself." I remember thinking what a damn good idea that was. I opened up and told him how I'd been doing decently but knew deep down I had been sheepish to take on new responsibilities because I wasn't confident in the processes, and the coding, and I had hit a plateau and was struggling to get to the next level of where I knew I needed to be.

I said, "I'm pretty good at the easier, more straightforward models, but when it gets more complex, I always get confused, especially when certain things are bundled together."

"Yeah, me too," he replied. "But reverse engineering has really helped me a lot. You should try it for yourself, I'll show you what I do."

I thanked him. That was rare in investment banking, and to be honest, it's rare just in general when it comes to the corporate world. The hypercompetitive nature of the corporate landscape makes more internal enemies than external ones at most firms.

I confessed to him, "Sometimes it's hard because I feel people expect more out of me because of my background. I am not sure if it's the expectations I still have of myself, but I feel like people look at me like I should be a robot and good at everything because of my first job."

I just remember he looked at me, and Reggie had this way of just making things better, lighter; there were no stressful situations when Reggie was around.

He said, "Sean, don't worry about stuff like that. You have a strong work ethic. We have a good team." Then he said something that has stuck with me, and I hold fast in my heart, "The cream always rises to the top."

It was a special moment because I did take Reggie's advice, and he did show me the way he learned through reverse engineering. Those models that were once a weakness became not just a strength in my career with his help, but to this day, that knowledge is the foundational technical skill set that has privileged me with many successes and achievements.

That's not the reason it was special, though. After a few years, we all went our separate ways in our careers. We stayed in touch. I had just seen Reggie. He had come to a pool party at my new home just a few weeks before I got a phone call out of the blue from Brandon—Reggie had passed away. Of all things, in a car accident. I still think about that. I remember being at his funeral. I'll always remember one of his friends who didn't make it out of Oak Cliff crying hysterically, the one I quoted earlier. He said, "Reggie had made it. Reggie had sacrificed so much to make it out, losing friendships when he left the area and when he started working in professional firms, wearing suits and ties. Reggie had always worked hard at academics, and no one could understand why. But now he could see why. That was Reggie's ticket out…"

I remember reflecting on the day of his funeral when the balloons were released into the air in his memory. Wondering why I was spared, but Reggie wasn't. I still think about it from time to time. I do not think I'll know the answer until I meet my Creator and see Reggie again, but it is a great reminder that life is fragile. No one knows when their time to go is. Stay focused, and move with integrity and urgency to accomplish your purpose, and no matter the circumstances or the odds, if they stand you up at the gates of Hell, don't back down.

CHAPTER 5

Burn the Ships

After a couple of years at the firm with Reggie and Brandon, I had a pretty good idea of what I wanted my future to look like, of what I believed, and still to this day do believe, is part of my unique purpose here on earth.

I began getting this vision of starting a business of my own, offering opportunities, growth, good compensation, and benefits for others. I started reading the autobiographies and biographies of other successful entrepreneurs, and I started noticing a lot of similarities between their psychology and my own. I began realizing one of my gifts is being a visionary. Even though I am a CPA and good with numbers, analysis, etc., there is this whole other side of me that is creative and loves to create art, content, stories, and poetry, and if I could draw or make music, I would do that, too! It became natural for me to see people and things not for where they currently were but for their future potential.

I wanted to build a business where I could lead, motivate, inspire, and create a place where my values could be instilled. Everyone has their own values, and the bigger a firm gets, the more corporate it, in some ways, almost has to become. I understand all those things, but I always wanted and still believe it can be done better.

As my purpose became more clear in my mind, I began to come to a crossroads. One of the things at that time was that I just had my undergraduate degree, and the regulations governing the prerequisites had been overhauled through the Sarbanes-Oxley legislation. I did not have enough college credit hours to sit for the CPA exam with the new law.

It may not sound like a big career change to go from banking to consulting, but most consulting firms are tied to accounting firms. In accounting, the CPA was and still very much is the gold standard. Now, I was lucky that at that firm, they valued work experience more than certifications and extra degrees. But being so young, having a vision of one day starting my own business, and not knowing what life may hold for me in the future, I began realizing I probably should get my CPA and probably do that while I was still single without the responsibilities of a family.

Ultimately, I decided it was best to go back to TCU to pursue a Master's degree so I could become CPA-eligible. The thought process was that with that certification down the line, I would be better equipped to be entrepreneurial and be able to pursue my purpose.

So much happened during that time at TCU—I met my wife, Sarah, and bought my first home. I ended up taking a job at a top ten global accounting and consulting firm, getting big-firm experience to complement the boutique firm experience, closed on my first home, became a CPA, and got engaged.

It was January 2018. My Dad took my whole family out to dinner, where we found out my Dad had just been diagnosed with stage 4 renal cell cancer. The prognosis was not good. The doctors estimated he had about six months to maybe a year to live. The relationship with my family and my parents is a little bit complex, like probably most people's. My parents had several small businesses that my dad actively managed, and obviously, with him being sick, they needed help taking care of those businesses so he could get treatments and focus on his health. I ended up leaving Grant Thornton in early 2018 to help my parents full-time.

For several months, I used that time to go around the businesses with my dad, learn how each is run, and helped him basically organize paperwork (what is it about the boomer generation not being organized—or is that just my parents?). Looking back, the decision to leave Grant Thornton at that time wasn't easy because I didn't quite feel like I was ready to be completely independent, and I did not feel like I had acquired enough experience or built the credibility and reputation yet to start my own business. Now, it helped to have a reason to help my family and get to share more time with my Dad when we had no idea how long he had left.

However, I was very sensitive to the fact that the world doesn't stop, and gaps in resumes can be red flags in the future. It had not been too long since my last experience when I left banking and struggled to find a job, and though I was doing a little bit of bookkeeping here and there for my parents, I wasn't gathering experience that would have been looked highly upon from many roles in my career.

I was about 26 at this point, and I remember being very thankful for the growth I had experienced through that time. It's these life moments and these decisions that ultimately end up defining your path. On one hand, I could choose to listen to the common sense of the world, living out of fear and living out of other people's expectations for me, and remained in my career and could have easily rationalized myself into that decision. There were people in my life who did care about me and gave me that advice (and while it is important to listen to a lot of people's perspectives when making big decisions, you ultimately must follow what you believe to be the best choice). Or I could take a step into the unknown again, trailblaze my own path, and live out my values. I always said, and still say, family before work; I think a lot of people say that. But there is a big difference between saying your values and walking in them through your actions.

This is where having an identity and purpose that are not based on some *thing* is vitally important. Though, it was not easy, it was easier to make this decision when I was confident that identity and purpose were not anchored to my job title. Moreover, this is also where the next steps of the fundamentals are hugely important. You must have concrete values you stand for that are unshakeable and a clear vision for your life. Put simply, you must have a high-definition, 8K resolution framed photo in your mind that answers the key question, how do you want your life to look?

Similarly to the framework involved with building your identity and purpose, your vision must not be anchored to *things* but rather to feelings and perceptions, your perceptions and those of others you respect. How I coach this concept is once a client is confident in their identity and purpose, we use their identity and purpose to come up with their own definition of success, and then we draft a personal *mission, vision,* and *values* statement. The mission is essentially the purpose rewritten, seemingly redundant. It's a worthwhile exercise because the more times it gets written out, the more clear it becomes. I feel like what helps people the most is, rather than explaining what and how to do these to give an example, so below is my personal *MVV* statement:

Mission: To lead and empower everyone in my sphere of influence to realize their full potential.

Vision: A life and legacy that reflects the character of Jesus Christ so powerfully that the manifestation of the Holy Spirit is undeniable and guides all called to salvation.

Values: Authenticity, Integrity, Accountability, Fortitude, Self-mastery, Wisdom, and Truth

The last piece of this exercise is to answer one simple yet difficult question—Why?

It is not exactly a trick question, but it is somewhat of a test. If you struggle to answer why, then you still have work to do. You need to keep reflecting, journaling, and crafting through your *MVV*. Your why might be the most powerful aspect of your journey because it's your why that will propel you through the adversity you will inevitably face. I don't make people share their why with me unless they feel inclined. The why is typically deeply personal and in some cases, wouldn't even be understood by anyone else. I'll share mine in hopes it might help inspire you.

Why? - I don't want others to have to experience all the same pain I did to learn the lessons I believe should be freely shared. I want to live a life of impact and value, and I know nothing is good apart from God. I want to be a husband, father, son, and brother my family can be proud of, and ultimately, I want everyone to share in the Kingdom of God.

Hopefully, you can see where having these concepts thought out and defined will help keep you centered and make better decisions. Now, my answers would have looked different back then, but they were defined well enough to guide me.

Lastly, these concepts should be used in every decision, not just big decisions. How we consider and deal with the little things in life, the daily frustrations, the quirks, and the small annoyances of others, shed a light onto our character and undoubtedly influence how we make big decisions for better or worse. The other amazing benefit to beginning this process, working on the fundamentals of your mindset to prime it for peak performance, and mastering yourself, is you will start seeing the great paradoxes of life. I think this is one of the reasons why Jesus spoke so often in parables.

What I mean by this is best illustrated by a reframing of the paragraph. The point about making sure to employ your *MVV* in all your decisions, even the small ones, could easily be restated that there are no big decisions, just a lot of small ones strung together. It's paradoxical in that the world will tell you a lot of things that are often exaggerated and dramatized things like:

"This is the biggest decision of your life!"

"Make sure you think through everything before making a decision as big as this one!"

"Doing that would kill your chances of ever having another job as good as the one you have now!"

I would guess you have probably heard something along those lines a time or two. And while some decisions may hold more weight than others, if we know ourselves, are confident in who we are and what we stand for, and are guided by those values in everything we do, then we will inevitably be gifted by default something else, perspective.

Here's the thing. While it was all true that leaving Grant Thornton at 26 to help my family was a risk, I was able to make that decision with the perspective of knowing that even if it did not work out, nothing was permanent in life. Challenges, mistakes, and even poor or bad decisions can all be overcome. The alternative, though seemingly more rewarding from a career and income perspective, was more permanent. It is a powerful ability to be able to be confident in all of your decisions no matter how others may perceive them or how against worldly wisdom they may seem to be when the majority of other people are living in spirits of doubt, fear, scarcity, lack, and make decisions based on fleeting emotions or which way the wind is blowing that day.

Alternatively, what is also paradoxical is that if I had gone against my core values and decided to stay in my career out of worldly wisdom, thinking that I needed to remain career-focused, it would have been a more costly, damaging, and permanent choice. How so, you might ask? Not only would I have missed out on extra time with my dad, but what I have realized is that when we act incongruently with our identities and values, we open the door to a mindset or spirit based on fear and doubt. It then becomes a slippery slope downward where even your everyday decisions (it always comes full circle) are viewed through the lens of a fear mindset. The more we move in fear, the further we drift from our values and our true selves. Although there is always a way back, it becomes increasingly difficult.

Most of us can think of times in our own lives when we made decisions against our values, and we can likely relate to how this creates a self-fulfilling prophecy. It becomes easier to continue down that path, and if it isn't you, then I am sure you have seen someone else experience this.

For me, it's balancing work and time with my family. I am by no means perfect, and there are days I work later than I should, but I am very careful not to make a habit of it. An example, once you stay late in the office once to get ahead it becomes easier to do it again and again (I do not want you to mistake me for saying that you should never work late or try to get ahead, but in this context, I know that spending time with my daughter and family is more important than a couple more hours of work. It all depends on the context and the season of life we're in).

The other key here is that each time you make progress, have a breakthrough, get promoted, level up in life, etc., there are new challenges and obstacles; many times, they appear larger than the last ones you just overcame. Being intentional with your decision-making process based on your *MVV* becomes its own self-fulfilling prophecy as well. As I have progressed through life, I have had multiple times where the circumstances seem insurmountable, but each time that I stayed true to my values, it all somehow worked out in my favor (personally, I credit these to God). Each time you see that take place in your life, it becomes easier and easier to stay true to yourself and have faith even through life's darkest moments and most challenging trials.

Lastly, once you make the decision to start your own personal transformation journey, it's important to stay steadfast, committed, and not look back. Sure, you may stumble, and you will make mistakes, but don't ever go back and undo all of the work you put in. There's a great history lesson that I think illustrates the mentality you should take when you start down this path.

When Cortes landed in the New World, he noticed his men were grumbling, and their attitudes were poor. Many were complaining and wanted to go back. Cortés was acutely aware of the implications of their waning morale. He knew that, in the face of the countless unknowns and dangers that lay ahead, a lukewarm attitude would undoubtedly mean failure and death. Success on their mission demanded not just physical strength but also unwavering resolve and a complete commitment to conquer all odds.

To galvanize his troops and transform their mindset and attitudes, he orders his men to burn the ships—their only lifeline and way back home. There was no going back. There were only two options: succeed or fail, live or die.

That was the mentality I adopted when I made the decision to help my family. I told myself, *I am doing this because it is what reflects my vision and core values. I will not look back, and no matter what happens, I can and will be successful in whatever I choose to do.* That's the mindset that must be adopted if you're going to be successful. That's the mindset that must be adopted when you make decisions—all of them, and especially the decision if you're serious about transforming your life and performing at your peak.

No more sort-ofs, kind-ofs, if I feel like it's, maybes, somedays, halfway. No more mediocrity, no more lukewarm attitudes, no more partial commitments. All those things will just lead to frustration and failure. So, ask yourself: *Are you ready to burn the ships?*

CHAPTER 6

Seize the Day

I remember in high school, I had an amazing U.S. history teacher. When we got into the subject of the American Revolution, he did an incredible job of painting the picture of what that room must have felt like as the founding fathers were getting ready to sign and ultimately sign the Declaration of Independence. He really drove home the idea of liberty and personal freedom. Personal independence was so important to these men that when they signed their names to that document, they were defying the king and the monarchy and staking not just their own lives, but the lives of their loved ones, their own fortunes, and their wealth. Every material thing, including their lives, was on the line once they signed that document.

There's a great quote by John Adams, "Always stand on principle, even if you stand alone."

Fortunately, in society today, independence, although still difficult to attain, isn't necessarily a life-or-death declaration. When I speak to independence and freedom, it can be defined in many ways, financial independence, or maybe it's geographic independence to live and be able to work where you want - one of the silver linings coming out of COVID is being able to work in a more remote environment and being able to travel or live in a different place and move around.

For me personally, I always think of independence as freedom over your time, schedule, and your system of values. It doesn't necessarily mean my definition needs to be the same as yours. But I know for me what that ultimately means is my desire and passion to be an entrepreneur and have autonomy in how I work when I work, the values which guide my work and the stewardship of assets, and have control over my schedule and my time.

I was fortunate that I had both big firm and small firm experiences, and when I left Grant Thornton the first time with the burn the ships mindset we discussed last chapter, I had no idea how all the different dots would all become connected, propelling me to a level of success I never thought attainable at such a young age.

One of my best mentors is Mr. Bob Gray. We met in 2016; we were both smokers, and we had the same schedule for smoke breaks. I'd seen him down there several times, and I struck up a conversation. He seemed like a good guy and worked in the same building. I just asked him what he did, who he worked for. He worked for a different accounting firm in the same building and worked in a similar role, not the exact same, but a similar line of business.

Next thing you know, he was inviting me to be part of his fantasy football league with other accountants and lawyers around the area. He invited me and my wife over to his annual Super Bowl parties. The relationship just developed naturally, organically. At one point, I reached out to him to grab lunch and mentioned to him that I'd left Grant Thornton to help take care of my family's businesses. It just so happened he was in a similar position. He had been a partner and recently retired. He and his wife had recently begun their own small practice in forensic accounting. He asked me if I wanted to work as an independent contractor and learn his line of business.

It was really neat how that organic, natural relationship turned into a great mentorship, but also a second professional discipline and expertise because I got to learn that business from the ground up. One thing that I didn't know at first but quickly found out was how much Bob was respected in his industry. As it turned out, he happened to be one of the most recognized forensic accountants in the world and had been a financial expert in a number of high-profile legal cases, and was heavily involved in the AICPA, even chairing the committee that drafted the updated guidance and professional standards as it relates to forensic accounting.

For almost five years, I owned my own little consulting shop and learned directly from Bob. We began growing together as business partners. After a couple of years and gaining more experience, Bob started taking me to different events, I got to speak at events and conventions at different CPA societies and was able to start branching out and securing different 1099 relationships with other larger firms. Not only was it amazing how everything came together, but I was also getting professional experience that no other firm could provide. I was working on high-profile, complex legal cases, building intricate, sophisticated models, and helping to draft excerpts of expert reports. I had control and autonomy over my schedule, spending more time with my wife, and then before I knew it, I was actually making more money out on my own than I had ever made as a W-2 employee and working fewer total hours overall.

Even more valuable than the amount of money I was able to make was the experience I was getting—I was running a business. I learned from Bob how to charge for my value and get paid accordingly. I observed how Bob communicated, learning when and how to deliver difficult messages. Bob taught me how to market and sell myself as an expert. I received a lot of great advice from Bob, and we continued to work together through COVID. In fact, 2020 was one of my most successful years as an entrepreneur. We were fortunate because forensic accounting is a natural hedge against economic risk. When M&A activity starts to decline, there tends to be more commercial litigation and a higher demand for forensic accountants. I earned $305,000 in 2020 when I was just 29 years old. I don't mention this to boast. Three years later, it's still my record income, and I use it solely as an illustration that it is possible to earn your value. It's possible to find success in a challenging and uncertain economy. It's possible to live a life consistent with your values, experiencing freedom, peace, and security. You don't have to work for a big firm or under a prestigious logo to achieve this.

However, I do realize that not everyone is cut out for entrepreneurship. So, if you are someone who is committed to building your career through a more traditional path, this part of the book is for you. Navigating a career in professional services is more difficult than it has ever been, in my opinion. COVID and remote/hybrid work environments have resulted in various consequences, some positive and some not so favorable. I'm not a workplace therapist, so I won't pretend to know all the consequences or solutions. But one thing I am sure of is that it has made entering the workforce and establishing yourself in your career during the first few years very challenging. Here are a few reasons why:

1. Firms run lean, and big firms are leaner than ever. That means almost everyone you work with is busy, many are overwhelmed and burnt out.

2. There are great silver linings to remote work, but it makes training and getting good experience more challenging, especially when those in the organization are not used to using technology the way millennials or Gen Z are.

3. Pair overwhelmed teams with hybrid/remote environments most new hires aren't getting high-quality training or experiences that lead to valuable growth.

Deloitte's latest *2023 Gen Z and Millennial Survey* reports some interesting statistics:

- "Nearly half of Gen Z (46%) and four in 10 (39%) of millennials say they feel stressed or anxious all or most of the time."

- "Gen Z and millennials are reporting increasingly high levels of burnout due to work-related pressures."

- "More than six in 10 Gen Z and around half of millennials have experienced harassment or microaggressions at work in the past 12 months."

Here's the other thing: in the professional services industry, the odds are already stacked against you. I'm not trying to discourage you, but I do believe that there should be more transparency about how it all works. So, don't shoot the messenger for sharing some of the insider knowledge that others might not. Outlined below are some of the rules of the game. This doesn't mean that there aren't exceptions, but for the most part, these are the truths that I learned the hard way. Hopefully, you won't have to go through the same difficulties:

- You are not hired with the hope or long-term plan that you will one day reach Partner. In fact, it's the opposite. You are hired for leverage and expected to leave after two to three years.

- No one, and I mean absolutely no one, cares about you or your career like you do (or should care).

- No workplace, team, or firm is a "family." Some may be more tight-knit than others. The terms may get thrown around, that's fine, but don't buy into it.

- Building on this, keep your personal life and friendships separate from your work. You may build some friendships at work, and that's great, but just know only a few friendships made in the workplace will stand the test of time. In fact, I would say most end the day one of you changes firms/jobs.

- Also, there will be some who come across as super friendly. Beware of those people; vet out their motives before trusting. One tip I learned is to always test people a few times. Come up with some things that are more private in nature, not career damaging, and that aren't true, and when you run into the super-duper friendly people who, for some reason, just want to know everything about you because you are so utterly fascinating to them tell them that thing in confidence and wait a couple of weeks and see how many other people find out about that thing that you told that person in confidence.

Do this more than a couple of times before giving trust. I had an experience like that and developed this method. When those types of people would come around, I would tell them something like, "Oh, I was late because my wife was having a really hard morning, she didn't get the promotion she was hoping for at work." Or "Yeah, I didn't do that XYZ task (I had done the task) because I ran out of time." This was always a great one because I had always completed the task, and if that person spread it around it made them look like a liar, gossip, and ultimately just a dumbass.

- At 99% of places, it really is all about the bottom line. All the other stuff—the one day a year you do community service, or whatever else, was literally all put into place for one of two possible reasons (or both):

  o The community service projects you work on are tied to a client and produce client goodwill and an ROI (return on investment).

- o Someone in HR crunched some numbers and read some data points that said something like "firms who give back to their communities are X% more profitable" and quantified the ROI.

- o Both of the above.

- At 99% of workplaces, the clients come first, always. Do not kid yourself. Some firms are more honest about it than others but do not drink the Kool-Aid.

- Your job is to make your boss look good, add to his/her bottom line, and make his/her life easy. Do not get that confused with anything else. If you are ever in a situation (not talking about ethical dilemmas), where you do not know what to do, just ask yourself: What would make my boss look good, add to the bottom line, and make their life easier? Do that.

- Stay in your lane. You will undoubtedly go into the workplace and notice right off the bat five to ten things you could instantly improve upon, make more efficient, innovate, etc. Unless you are in a rare culture, or it's explicitly asked and in your job description—just don't do it. What will happen is the person who is in charge of whatever thing you are making better will feel threatened. They will talk to so and so, and so and so will talk to ABC, and ABC will talk to XYZ until it comes all the way back around to bite you right in the ass. No good deed goes unpunished in Corporate America.

- Make sure you read every single word of your employment agreements. It's worth the $500 to $1,000 to have an attorney review them before you sign anything as well.

- o If nothing else, you need to know the amount of ownership they are taking over you. I am not exaggerating; most employment agreements, especially as you move up, will say things like, "In exchange for your time, abilities, talent, intellectual property, and anything you do while employed by the firm, we agree to compensate you $X."

- o Make no mistake, they are buying you. Fortunately, we have not gone full *1984* (you should read that book, too), and they can't claim ownership over ideas in your mind. If you come up with a good idea that you may want to explore one day on your own— keep it to yourself. Do not *do* anything with it. If it is something that could be valuable, you will have to leave and explore that opportunity, or else risk the firm claiming ownership over whatever that product or service may be.

If you have not read Robert Greene's *48 Laws of Power,* you are doing yourself an injustice, especially if you are going into professional services. It is a must-read for your career, especially if you aspire to climb the corporate ladder.

By now, I am sure some of you think I am heavily biased. I won't deny my biases, but I assure you that is the blunt, cold, hard truth, and I can explain why that is the case. The reason those points seem so bleak and depressing is that professional services firms, especially the ones with the traditional Partnership operating model, are built on a structure of misaligned incentives. Crazy, right? One of the first things you learn in your first management class in business school is the importance of aligning incentives. How could that even be possible for some of the largest firms in the world that they could survive in 2023 with misaligned incentives?

I'll explain in the traditional operating models, there are essentially three levels to the pyramid.

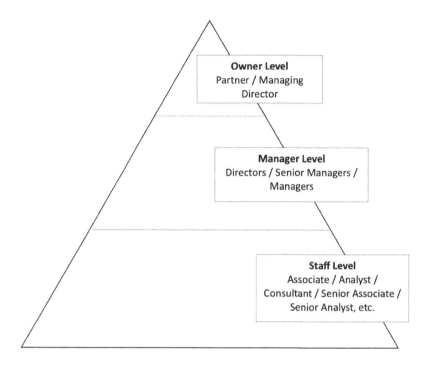

Now, there are different roles and titles at each level, and there is nuance, but overall, that is the model. Here's the catch—each level has different incentives, and by different, I mean opposing incentives. Yes, as backward, inefficient, and honestly stupid as it sounds, the teams themselves that go to work in the trenches together have incentives that oppose each other.

As a staff (if your title is anything along the lines of Associate, Analyst, Senior Associate, Senior Analyst, Consultant, Senior Consultant, you are typically on staff level), your end-all, be-all metric is utilization. Utilization is simply the number of hours you bill (chargeable to clients) divided by the standard hours of your firm—typically around 2,000.

As a manager (if your title is Manager, Experienced Manager, Senior Manager, and Director, you are on this level). If any Senior Managers/Directors are reading this, I know what you're thinking, and I hate to break it to you, but I was a Director, too. I get it, it's a fun title, but let's not kid ourselves; you don't have equity. It's still a glorified manager at the end of the day. Your incentive is to hit your utilization metrics but also to manage the budget, aka, make sure the staff under you do not bill more hours than what was agreed upon when winning the work. Now, this level is more nuanced than the others depending on the title, and to throw the Senior Managers/Directors some credit on top of managing the budgets, you are also expected to manage client relationships, originate revenue, and basically do anything and everything possible to prove you are worthy of the partnership.

As a partner (if your title is Partner, Principal, or Managing Director, you are on this level), your incentive is to originate as much revenue as possible, manage and expand client relationships, and manage your P&L. Yes, the partner P&L is basically the revenue from projects you originate less the time billed by the team to complete the project. There are levels to the partnership, but that is not the point of this book and would likely be a book on its own.

Hopefully, by now, you see what I mean when I say the incentives oppose each other. Though you work for the same firm, you are quite literally not on the same team. Now, in good times, this structure is less of an issue; like I said, it's nuanced. Some partners are better leaders than others. Some firms are more metric-driven than others. But when times are tough, when the economy is in a recessionary environment, those metrics tend to mean everything. You don't have to take my word for it. Most of the large public accounting firms had RIFs (reductions in force, layoffs) earlier in 2023. Ask around, search forums, and *Reddit*. Most firms picked a utilization threshold, and anyone under that threshold was laid off. Again, this is high level. There is a little more nuance to those decisions but do not be misled at the staff and manager level to some extent, the decision was largely based on utilization.

Basically, until you make the partnership level, you are always stuck in an endless dilemma between utilization metrics and making your boss happy – remember that rule – make your boss happy? The incentive structure makes it even more difficult than it should be.

Here's the good news, if this is the game you want to play, I have the advice and strategy to win even though the statistics, current circumstances, and structure are all slanted against you. I already put a lot of my high-level advice in the bullet points above, but the key here is a step-based process (these are also applicable to other corporate jobs):

Step One: Know who you are (we've gone into detail on all of this already).

Step Two: Acknowledge the truth, don't drink the Kool-Aid, and keep everything in perspective. It's a job, that's it, don't make it your identity (ironically, in the same Deloitte *2023 Gen Z and Millennial Survey* referenced earlier in the chapter it reports 49% of Gen Z and a whopping 62% of millennials see their work as *central* to their identity—no wonder so many are unhappy). Basically, acknowledge the bullet points I laid out earlier, if your firm has a slightly better culture or you're blessed to work with a great boss, that is awesome. Those things can change, though, so again, figure out where your situation falls into the mix from the points above and acknowledge the game is against you, not for you.

Step Three: Become an excellent human being. Essentially, don't be the gossip, don't be the backstabber. Become known as the person in your team with the most integrity. Put other people before yourself.

Step Four: Be experience-driven, not money or title driven. Take on the hard projects, ask for more challenging work, and deal gracefully with difficult clients. Your true value will be tied to the experiences you successfully complete, not your title or salary.

Step Five: Leverage steps three and four to build a vast internal and external relationship network. By being an excellent, high-integrity person and taking on challenges with a good attitude, people will be naturally drawn to you. Remember, these aren't your family or your best friends, as I am not contradicting myself but build those relationships appropriately.

Step Six: Do favors for people early on. Try to make them small favors, I don't want you falling into the trap of becoming a "yes" person, but this is chess, not checkers. It's like poker. Rather than stacking up chips, stack up favors, especially with peers and direct managers. Try your best not to ask for favors, and when you do, always trade value for value; as an example, I have a lot of great relationships with investment bankers, and I did sometimes need favors from them. Every time I asked them for a favor, I came to them with something of value they could use, too. In Corporate America, successful businesses and relationships are built on mutual value.

Step Seven: You must be patient and long-term oriented. You will undoubtedly be passed up for a promotion or not get credit where it should have been given. Bad things happen. If you want to win at this game, you must be playing the long game. It's a marathon, not a sprint.

Step Eight: Leverage steps five through seven. Become a leader. It does not necessarily need to be a title, though title does become important in this process. By this point, by employing the steps I have laid out, you should be somewhere on the manager level. If you are doing all these steps plus the fundamentals from earlier on you will already have a natural following. Mentor and develop people on the levels below you. Take extra time to make sure they get the training and experiences they need to be successful. Develop relationships with them and take an interest in who they are as people. If you do this right, you will begin accumulating influence and power.

Step Nine: Figure out what you want. Maybe that's equity and becoming a partner, maybe it's more autonomy or a special project, maybe it's a career change into an industry with high barriers to entry like private equity. Figure out who in your firm has the ability to get what you want. Build the relationships necessary and keep stacking the political and leadership clout to position you to get what you want.

Step Ten: Ruthlessly, and I mean ruthlessly, go get what you want. Remember, these steps are slow, I would say in a traditional big four accounting firm, each step would represent a year. By year ten, employing these strategies, many of you may have already gotten what you want. But if you didn't, just remember power is not given, it is taken. You may be in a situation where you will have to put all your chips on the table and go all in for what you want. I will say at this point, you will likely have accumulated more power than many people in your firm regardless of title, so don't be scared.

There are a couple of other important keys here. You must be constantly learning new skills, working on soft skills, developing your leadership, and maybe most importantly, developing strong sales/negotiating skills with a high emotional IQ and executive presence. There are a lot of great books on sales, negotiating, emotional IQ, and executive presence, and although they are different concepts, there is significant overlap between them all. The ability to read a room, sell services, negotiate, and command respect among C-suite executives is by far the most important skill that sets me apart.

It is impossible to lay out everything in a book, and that is why training and working with mentors and coaches is so important. More likely than not, you will probably need to invest in yourself to find those resources. I invested over $50,000 this past year in my own self-development, and it's not to brag, only to illustrate. I wanted to be the best, so I wanted to learn from the best. The best bring a ton of value, and they deserve to be paid on their value, and it was worth every single penny.

Entrepreneurs and others—I did not forget about you! The process is pretty much the same for you; the only difference is that you are likely in a game where some of the circumstances are more in your favor. The keyword here is "some." Although you probably won't have to deal with misaligned incentives, some of the other aspects regarding work environment and culture are hopefully healthier. And if you're starting a business, you probably have some experience and are not starting at step one. Let's not beat around the bush—starting a business is hard. Statistically, the odds are that your business will fail. However, while I cannot make any guarantees, the steps are the same; they just lean more externally focused.

I would hope and advise that if you are starting a business, you already have a strong business relationship network. Essentially, focus on steps six through ten with an emphasis on sales skills, negotiations, leadership, emotional IQ, executive presence, and self-investment. Concentrate on building mutual value; if you can provide value to someone or some business, you can be successful. The key is to be able to communicate that value and secure the first sale. I don't care how many times you get told "no"; keep selling until you find your first "yes." I promise it's all downhill after the first win.

I know I've laid out a lot in this chapter. It was purposeful; I wanted to make sure I actually included some real substance in this book. These are things I wished people had told me early on in my career. The reason they don't is that the truth is hard to hear, and many of the people who know what I know are now benefiting from the system and continue to perpetuate it for no other reason than because that's "just how it is" or because "that's what [they] went through to earn [their] stripes."

The difference is just because I went through something doesn't mean I think others should too. And just because society did something one way for a long time doesn't mean that it can't be improved or changed for the better. All I ask is that you pay it forward. If you read this and it helps you, make sure that at some point, you pass the knowledge on to someone else and help them too.

Lastly, I want to emphasize the significance of the two words: patience and process. The steps and advice in this chapter are not meant to be employed all at once or even right after one another quickly. Look at them as guides and principles for building some foundational career philosophies, and make sure to make them your own. Interpret them your way, employ them as naturally as possible and in your own unique style; remain authentic and true to yourself. For example, I spoke about leadership—it's important, but there are a million different ways to be a good leader. Find a style you like and develop it in your own way. We discussed the importance of networking and building relationships—ensure that those occur organically and grow at their own speed.

Overall, each and every day will present new challenges and new opportunities. Take everything you've learned and approach each day with strategy, confidence, and alignment with your vision. If you do that long enough with consistency, you will be successful. Seize the day.

CHAPTER 7

Be My Escape

I did intentionally keep one key item out of the last chapter as it related to the steps of building a successful business from an entrepreneurial standpoint–scale. Scale is the one important key ingredient my first entrepreneurial venture lacked.

Forensic accounting is a very specialized skill set. Professional services, in general, is a specialized skill set, and large firms with established logos dominate the industry. I am not going back on what I said earlier, logos and prestigious brands are not the end-all, be-all as it relates to a career, but from an entrepreneurial perspective, it's a barrier to entry and a barrier to scale.

There's a reason you don't see a ton of start-ups in the professional services industry, and the ones you do see tend to be niche, boutique firms that carve out a small market share of their own. It's not impossible to scale in the industry, but it does require a fair amount of capital that needs to be invested in talent. I had plans to scale and build my small consulting practice.

Heading into 2020, I had saved up a nice chunk of change. I was working on a plan to lease a small office space, and I was in the process of looking into creating a paid internship program to develop a young associate and hopefully hire them full-time. And just like Steinbeck said, "The best-laid plans of mice and men often go awry." The COVID pandemic turned the world and, for a while, my life upside down.

It was November 2020. I was actually on the golf course, and it was so strange. I felt completely normal when I woke up and started the round, but around the 12th hole, I got up to hit my tee shot and was overcome with a feeling of lightheadedness mixed with dizziness. I took a few moments, sipped some water, and thankfully it passed. Then a couple of holes later, I felt it again, but this time I didn't say anything. I was with some friends, and I did not want to freak anyone out. Fortunately, I was able to finish the round, and when I got home, I was feeling absolutely exhausted. I thought, well, I woke up early and played some golf. I don't typically feel this tired after golf. But truth be told, during the height of the COVID pandemic, I had gotten a little bit lazy. And during the lockdowns, we had ordered out too much, and I had probably put on 30 or 40 pounds, which was not great. I had recently been working on getting myself back into shape and thought maybe the increased exercise had just gotten to me more than I thought.

I remember I went to bed earlier than usual, and the next morning I woke up, and my throat was on fire. That's the only way I know how to describe it; it was the worst pain I had ever felt in my throat. Like a typical man, I tried to play it off cool, but my wife suggested I use one of our at-home COVID test kits.

"Why don't you take one?"

"Okay, I really don't think it's COVID. I'm not coughing. I don't feel anything in my chest, but I'll take it so we can be sure."

I took the test, and sure enough, it read positive for COVID. I thought, I don't know, though. I'm not coughing, and the verdict was still out on how accurate the at-home tests were. I decided to go to the local urgent care and get a second test. I tested positive for COVID.

At that time, my daughter wasn't even a full year old, and there were more questions than answers regarding COVID. Out of an abundance of caution, I had my wife and daughter leave to go stay with family. My health began deteriorating very quickly. Fortunately, I did not have to go to the hospital. But on the third night, I got really close. It felt like I couldn't breathe, and what was really strange was the only reason I didn't go to the hospital was that I'd called my doctor and, based on their recommendation, I had ordered one of the little gadgets that you put on your finger that tells you how much oxygen you have from Amazon the day before; even though it felt like I couldn't breathe, I still had 98% oxygen. How that works—I am not sure I'll ever know. It was a rough two weeks; it took me a full 11 days before I felt any semblance of normal health again, and eight days before I kicked the fever (I almost never get fevers, and when I do, that usually means I am really sick).

I know I am likely not the only one who got COVID, and I know it could have been worse. I tell the story because it took me a very long time to fully recover. For the few months right after, it was just day after day of barely being able to get out of bed. I remember trying to do one thing a day. If I could manage one thing, whether it was working a little bit, doing a household chore, or taking care of my daughter, I considered it a productive day. I recall having to take daily naps, which is not necessarily a bad habit, but I hadn't needed them so often before. I also noticed small changes in my brain. I was slower, my focus wasn't as sharp, and I had a hard time paying attention to things, even just watching a movie or TV. Over time, I discovered I wasn't the only one who experienced some of these things. I guess the technical term for it is "Long COVID." I dealt with the effects for about six months before I fully recovered, which I am grateful for, as I have heard there have been cases where people are still feeling the ramifications of Long COVID.

Going through something like that, you begin to realize that you can't take your health for granted. I also firsthand saw how your mindset, mental health, and physical health are intertwined. I ultimately believe I made a full recovery because I was mentally determined to do so.

I remember on the days when I had a little bit of energy, I would force myself to go outside for walks to get sunlight and some light exercise. Losing my sense of taste and smell did kick-start a diet because I wasn't interested in eating much. Not saying that's the greatest way to start a diet, but fortunately, it was a bit of a silver lining for me. It took me losing considerable weight, redesigning my diet around healthy, whole, nutritious foods, and exercising to finally get back to full health.

Not only is your health extremely important in life, but it's also crucial for peak performance, and it's hugely significant in business, especially if your business isn't scaled. During that time period, it was questionable how I was going to make money and provide for my family. It was by God's grace that I had just finished a large project, and I happened to get paid enough money to last us a year or so if we had to stretch it that long. I was fortunate to have all that time to essentially focus on my health. However, it's not always guaranteed that something bad will happen when it's most convenient for you financially. In fact, I have read and heard many stories of entrepreneurs losing successful businesses due to a health crisis or long-term illness.

Most people long for routines. We try to build habits and processes that minimize risk and maximize our value and productivity. All of these are good, but here's the thing—life can and will throw you curveballs. Going through this ordeal was a bit of a wake-up call for me. I needed to find a way to scale my business so that when another curveball was thrown at me, I could continue to provide for my family.

By this point, COVID had upended so many things about work, and there was little certainty about anything, so my original plans to lease office space and hire an intern didn't make much sense anymore. I decided that I should capitalize on the opportunities at hand to maximize earnings and then reassess my strategy when there was more certainty about the future of the workplace post-COVID. Fortunately, my background in healthcare transactions was valuable, and the healthcare M&A market was booming in 2021. The big firms had made sizable layoffs at the beginning of the pandemic in 2020 (remember what I said about when times are bad), and the market was at a standstill for a few months. Those two factors combined, and I could take on contract work with almost any firm of my choosing.

I took on a contract with Grant Thornton in their healthcare M&A group. I already knew their templates, and styles, and was familiar with the team, so it was an efficient choice where I could get plugged in quickly and maximize my hours and bill rates as a contractor. It was a challenge, don't get me wrong, but managing the stress from the workload is way easier when you're getting paid by the hour, there's an end date to your contract, and you have control over whether you extend your contract or move on.

Ultimately, I excelled in the role to the point where I was offered a full-time position, which I first respectfully declined. I want to emphasize again the importance of negotiating, the ability to read the room, and knowing who holds power and leverage. I declined the offer for a lot of reasons. At a high level, the offer was unsolicited, meaning they came to me without me asking for an offer. Reading between the lines, that's an indication of who holds the leverage – in this case, I held the leverage. The next part is even more important: your greatest negotiating tactic is the ability to walk away. To put this differently, never negotiate if you are unwilling to say no and walk away. If you do, just know that's not a negotiation; that's you getting steamrolled. Don't worry, I have been steamrolled my fair share of times.

The other reason I said no is that I didn't want what they were offering. I had just worked for over three months straight and made almost the entire salary they offered me on a short-term contract. As a contractor, you will almost certainly always make more money. The downsides are that there is more risk (short-term), you pay more in taxes, you have to get health insurance and benefits on your own, and typically you will be put on the worst projects with the worst clients, and probably have little to no support (which is also an advantage because that typically means you bill more time). Moreover, I had proven myself more capable than almost all the other Directors they had, so why would I accept a position lower than my value? Always make sure you get paid based on your value.

Lastly, negotiating is a lot like dating. Think back to high school and college. If you asked someone out on a date and they said no, did that make you more or less interested in that person? Saying no to an offer doesn't shut the door; oftentimes, it just makes the other party more interested. Ultimately, the negotiations went on for at least six months, and I was offered a pretty good package. It wasn't exactly what I had wanted, but it checked a lot of the boxes, and I did decide that it would be valuable to get some experience as a leader. I accepted a full-time offer back at Grant Thornton later that year.

It was hard putting an end to a successful entrepreneurial experience. It was the right decision because of the people I met and the relationships I made. There was a part of me, too, that felt like I had some unfinished business, and the fact that everything had come full circle back to the same job I had left years earlier to help my family was now asking me to come back and be a leader in their practice, build out a team, give me autonomy over my work, and promise bigger opportunities down the line. After dealing with COVID, being responsible for a young family, and still facing lingering uncertainty in the world, a little bit more consistency and stability did not sound like an entirely bad escape.

CHAPTER 8

High Hopes

Things were going well. Within a year back at Grant Thornton, I was promoted to Director (that was the one box left unchecked when I first started). I did get to straddle two service lines as I had negotiated, and I had just finished testifying as a named expert witness. Don't get me wrong, things were not perfect, and some of the things I had negotiated for never really came to fruition, but that's life. You win as many battles as possible and play the long game.

2022 was winding down, and I admit it; up to this point, I was an AI (artificial intelligence) denier. Sure, the easy things would be able to automate and make more efficient, but my job is so complex. Every business, every transaction – they are all so different, there's no way my job could be automated. Fortunately, technology has always interested me, and I at least kept up with things. In November of 2022, I saw a headline that caught my eye, detailing some things Google was doing with neural networks and machine learning.

Now, many people think ChatGPT is AI. It is a form of AI, and while it is impressive, it is just an aspect of AI. What really started piquing my curiosity was the engine that powered AI – the machine learning algorithms. Google was automating complex processes with its machine learning algorithms.

I had also recently innovated several of our services on my team at GT and unlocked more efficiency and greater precision in complex analyses. As I read more and more about machine learning models, it began to dawn on me – my job can be automated. Maybe not 100%, but well into the 60% to 80% range. I thought if my job can be automated, then my team and I should sure as hell be the ones to automate it and benefit from the technology rather than be replaced and devalued by it.

What began as a hobby quickly turned into a dedicated commitment because the more I learned, the more I realized the fullness of the disruption we are just beginning to see manifest currently. I was both fascinated and scared. By March, when the proliferation of generative AI began unfolding with the launch of OpenAI's first iteration of ChatGPT, I was working from 6 or 7 am in the morning to typically 9 or 10 pm at night (I would take a two-hour break in the evening to have dinner and spend time with my family), and then once I finished my work responsibilities, I would sign on to Udemy, Coursera, or get on Codefinity and go through self-learning modules on AI, machine learning, and software development courses – many nights until 3 am in the morning.

One of the reasons I don't believe in coincidences is because if you remember the beginning of the book when I detailed going through the period of lost focus and finding the Flow Research Collective. I could use the strategies I learned from the FRC to absorb the knowledge quickly by being in the flow state (learning to harness the power of flow is ultimately one of the advantages of building habits of peak performance but is more advanced and nuanced and is best learned through a more structured coaching platform. To learn more flow-specific research through reading, I suggest *The Rise of Superman* by Steven Kotler and *Flow* by Mihaly Csikszentmihalyi). By April 2023, about three months of dedicated learning into the early morning hours, I was proficient at what I needed to be.

I had this grand vision of using what I had learned to make our jobs and lives easier at Grant Thornton. I had strategies laid out in my mind, use cases, and had shared some of which I learned with colleagues at Grant Thornton to help position us for the future. I knew, though to capitalize we must move with urgency because what we are witnessing today regarding advancements in AI and machine learning is exponential. It has appeared to have plateaued a little bit (not enough to become complacent) but essentially what I mean is that time period of April through June 2023 when every day a new AI service was coming out, some of them literally just a better version of a service that was no more than a day or two old, was symbolic of what we used to believe would take years of advancement. Put simply, what used to take years now takes a day such that time, correlated to technological advancements, is speeding up to a pace the human mind can quite comprehend.

Probably many of you had to read a book in high school or at least have heard of a book by Charles Dickens called *A Tale of Two Cities*, and know of the famous quote, "It was the best of times, it was the worst of times." That is the best summary of my personal thesis for what we are going to experience in the next decade as it relates to advances in artificial intelligence, machine learning, and automation.

I do believe the best way to illustrate this is that reality itself is going to become more disparate, especially economic reality. There will be people who have been keeping up with the advancements, people like me who jumped in and absorbed as much as they possibly could to stay on the curve, and those with remaining time left who will end up being able to capitalize on an opportunity that is greater than but can only be likened to the Industrial Revolution. Sadly, there will also be those who remain content and comfortable with the status quo and hold on to their "horse and buggy," rather than investing in a Model-T.

It dawned on me when I was helping a former colleague look for a new job after being laid off. I went to Deloitte's website to search for their open positions for him, and immediately, I noticed there was almost no mention of the word accounting or CPA. I think on the home screen it mentioned the word "audit" only once, and it was in the context of an AI audit. Deloitte has always been a very technology-driven firm, but it's also one of the big four accounting firms. When I noticed that, it really hit me that the skill sets that are valuable in the disruptive, transitioning economy are very different from the skill sets that many of us have. Even the few open positions for traditional roles like audit manager had desired requisite experience in cloud computing, AI-based platforms, and some listed SQL and Python coding languages.

I could be wrong, but I do not believe the economy is in a traditional recession. I do not think the forces driving the market are cyclical; I think they are transformational. For example, by trade, I'm a CPA. One of the reasons I became a CPA was because it was a pragmatic approach to a career and provided job security for my future. That's not to say that the knowledge I gained becoming a CPA isn't still valuable, but the channels and mediums through which we present that knowledge to clients are no longer the high-value channels of communication. I imagine many of you reading this book are proficient in Microsoft Excel spreadsheets and creating presentations in Microsoft PowerPoint. These are what I would call static environments, meaning that once the spreadsheet is populated and the presentation is made, they don't change unless you manually update them. That's no longer a very high-value deliverable to clients. If focused effort isn't made to self-invest, self-learn, and upskill, I do think you are putting your skill set at massive risk of becoming obsolete, no matter your current role, title, skill set, or paycheck.

As I mentioned when I was helping my friend who got laid off, the RIFs (Reduction in Force) are already taking place. There were other signs too, pointing to the fact that the current volatility of the economy and capital markets is being driven by disruptive, transformational changes rather than the more well-known cyclical forces (like most things in life, I acknowledge it is a mixture of both, but my hypothesis is that the primary driver is disruptive, foundational shifts). Out of respect for my former colleagues and firm, I won't go into greater detail about some of the other empirical pieces of evidence that formed the basis of my thoughts on the current economic forces at play. I will say, however, that I decided to leave my job at GT to become more prepared for the new economy that is already being unveiled before our very eyes.

I started a custom machine learning and AI business and also launched my coaching platform, called Resonate, after this book. One of the premier coaching programs is called "Future-proof" (named after my second book that I am currently working on and will go into greater detail on advancements in AI). I am passionate about helping others, and I don't want people to have to stay up until 3 a.m. for months on end to self-learn these skills.

Since I did not have the opportunity to coach my former colleagues on these platforms, I am going to do it through Resonate. What's amazing about having a vision, staying true to your values, and creating mutual value is that I was afforded a partnership that allows me to provide members who take the "Future-proof" course access to a state-of-the-art machine learning and AI platform that costs approximately $200,000, and personally teach them how to use it, create their own machine learning algorithms, and give them a hugely valuable technical skill set they can add to their resumes and generate more earning power and value for themselves.

I don't write any of this to scare you, but I am honest, brutally honest when I believe it's necessary (if you can read between the lines and connect some dots from this chapter back to chapter six, you probably understand better now why my bullet points around professional services firms did not sugar coat anything). The good news is, if you are willing to invest time, effort, and resources to learn new things, you should not be scared at all but rather excited. The barriers to entry have never been lower, and we are entering a time filled with massive opportunities. With a commitment to the principles of this book, we should all be filled with optimism and high hopes.

CHAPTER 9

Lux Aurumque

One of my favorite quotes is from Aristotle.

"Excellence is never an accident. It is always the result of high intention, sincere effort, and intelligent execution."

It represents the wise choice of many alternatives. Choice, not chance, determines your destiny. It might be one of the most complete and perfect quotes that I've ever read. It lays out the process of finding success or excellence. It emphasizes the need to have the wisdom to focus on one thing while sacrificing other alternatives, and lastly, it also speaks to the right mindset of taking ultimate accountability for yourself. Your future, your destiny, and your current situation are based on your choices, not any type of circumstance. In a way, that quote has inspired the system of principles that I've put in place. Throughout the book, I've shared some of my past experiences, successes, achievements, failures, and mistakes, all of which we're bound to encounter. The beauty of my system (and my faith) is that there's grace and forgiveness built in. When you make mistakes but consistently act in accordance with the principles and your core values, those mistakes can be overcome, and it's arguable they aren't really mistakes but rather learning experiences.

I can say with confidence that the principles combined with my personal experiences and the neuroscience behind the process and habits laid out, when used consistently over a sufficient period of time, will guarantee a sense of purpose and fulfillment in your life. Now, you may have noticed we didn't delve heavily into the RESONATE acronym yet, and that was intentional for two reasons.

The first reason is that to properly apply principles in any discipline, you must first have a strong foundation and master the fundamentals. The fundamentals related to peak performance involve defining your identity, purpose, mission, vision, values, and why. There is more nuance that we briefly touched on throughout the book, including building routines, meditation, journaling, visualization, eliminating distractions, getting daily sunlight, hydrating, and fueling your body with a healthy diet. I didn't want to waste your time by going in-depth on these subjects because they should be tailored to each individual, and there are already hundreds, if not thousands, of books that explain these concepts, along with many free resources available online (I also assume that if you picked up this book, you are already familiar with and implementing some of these practices in your life).

The second reason is that, although the acronym was not explicitly highlighted in the text, it was woven into my story. And let's face it, stories are more engaging and enjoyable. On average, we learn better through stories, and if I've been able to hold your attention this far in the book, it's likely because you found some interest in my story. I highly doubt anyone would have read this far if I had taken a textbook-style approach to explaining the meaning of the RESONATE acronym.

Like the quote by Aristotle, everything that manifests itself into physical reality begins in the mind as a thought, idea, or intention. Those intentions, if something we choose to bring our awareness to, to focus on, something we believe in and have faith in, and something we value, naturally inspire us to take action, which is the physical component. The belief that motivates us beyond the mind to persevere in the action is the spiritual component.

There are many definitions of what peak performance is or what it looks like. For me, I define peak performance as the harmony or resonance, if you will, where mind, body, and spirit are working together in coherence, enabling us to push past what we believe to be our limits. With that understanding, my principles become easier to comprehend and apply.

Rhythm:

There is a natural rhythm to everything in the world. Each day has its own rhythm. The golf swing has a rhythm. We have our own natural biorhythms which govern the different times of day when we are more naturally energized and productive (that's why some people exercise early in the morning and others late at night).

Connecting back to my story, I didn't start back at Grant Thornton as a Director; it wasn't my title in the beginning. However, I led and acted in rhythm as if I were one. The ability to become aware of each day's rhythm, especially in the context of my time back at GT, afforded me the ability to lead teams and earn respect without the need to be dictatorial or overbearing. I knew when it was time to hit the gas and when it was time to hit the brakes. The people under your leadership appreciate when you have insight and sensitivity to the overall mood and attitude of the team. This skill alone can take you far in life.

Find your rhythm and be in tune with the rhythm of others. Begin to notice small daily shifts in your own rhythm and in others. Act in accordance with this principle, and things will take shape more naturally and with less effort. If you want to test this principle, go hit some golf balls.

Try to swing the club as fast as you can and hit the ball as far as you can. Next, swing naturally, with rhythm. Which swing resulted in better outcomes?

Did the ball go farther when you tried really hard to hit it far, or did it go farther when your swing felt slower but had rhythm? Remember, life is a big paradox, and you can achieve better results with less effort.

Emotion:

Emotion has a double meaning. The first is straightforward. We are emotional as humans, and I am not a believer in suppressing or ignoring emotions. Our emotions are signals that give us awareness of what is happening in our minds and bodies; they are extremely important. However, we should make sure we are using our emotions to work for us and not against us. Take the time to work out your own emotional baggage (we all have it). If you have not already, learn to become the master of your emotions and not the other way around.

During my time back at GT, I was coaching a colleague who had just come through a very poor experience with another person on the team. His attitude and mindset were not in a great place, but he had such great potential. I remember he had done some really good work leading a complex project during a busy period when there wasn't much time to give him much feedback or attention. He did an excellent job leading the project almost single-handedly, but he was still young and it took him a lot of time to be able to do what he did, and he billed those hours (which was the right thing for him to do). The amount of time he charged ruffled some feathers, and he received an email from a partner asking for an explanation.

He was about to explode. Fortunately, for him, he vented his emotions to me. I told him there are ways to communicate what you're feeling that will help you rather than hurt you. Essentially, I helped him craft an email that was overly detailed, respectful, and borderline obnoxious, almost (but not quite) to the point of being sarcastic. The email took those emotions and reframed them in a way that was productive, rather than destructive to his career. He has gone on now to become a Manager and received a 40% raise less than a year out from when I helped him craft that email.

The other part of emotion is developing a high emotional IQ. This takes time and practice. You can read about it, but over time, mastering your emotions will make you better at reading other people's emotions. It is rooted in awareness and attention to detail. Pay attention to non-verbal clues, and read people's mannerisms and facial expressions. High emotional IQ may be the most important differentiator and is one of the skills that is most highly correlated with becoming an executive leader – at least, according to research performed by *Harvard Business Review*.

Sequence:

Conversely to emotion, there is sequence, in the context of these principles, meaning logic. Everything has a sequence. The way I was able to learn machine learning algorithms was by understanding the sequence, or computer logic, behind building the algorithms. It's also how I concluded that my job could be automated and changed my mind about AI. Everything we do can be distilled into a big "if," "when," "and," "or," "then" statement. Think about it, and name anything you do. For example, getting a glass of water:

If: I am thirsty.

Then: I go to the cabinet;

And: Get an empty glass.

Then: I fill the empty glass with water;

And: Drink the water.

The better logic and sequencing you have, the better you will become at your craft. It doesn't just apply to technical skill sets, either. There is a sequence to soft skills. For example, knowing the proper sequence of how to network and communicate, from the introduction stage to the engagement around small talk, to piquing curiosity and interest, to relating to that person on an emotional level, through the follow-up and ongoing cultivation of the relationship. This type of soft skill sequence is what Bob was so good at and one of the greatest lessons I ever learned from him.

Superior sequencing is definitely a valuable differentiator. Superior sequencing paired with high emotional intelligence is an absolute game changer.

Order:

I know what you may be thinking, *Aren't order and sequence the same thing?* No, in the context of the RESONATE principle, order refers to the hierarchy in any given situation. Whether you like it or not, whether you agree or not, despite your feelings about authority and people with power, you must respect the order of things, especially in large institutions and organizations.

The steps I laid out in Chapter Six, specifically the bullet point about your job being centered on making your boss look good, are the result of the principle being put into practice. There are times when the order or hierarchy probably should be redesigned or struck down entirely. However, unless you are placed into a position of power and influence to accomplish that kind of objective, it is not in your best interest to critique the order of things.

If you have a hard time respecting the hierarchy in a given situation, that is likely a sign that you need to move on and away from that situation or place. Destruction of order, even with the best intent, typically leads to even worse conditions. A few historical examples include Reconstruction after the U.S. Civil War, the French Revolution, the Russian Revolution, Mao's Cultural Revolution in China, and the list goes on.

If you feel the need to change the order of things (which I can certainly relate to), I advise building something new rather than trying to tear it down and replace something old. For example, if you do not like the institutional order of your job, start your own company. If you are not entrepreneurially minded or not ready, no one is forcing you to stay there, and trust me, going against the established order in a large organization is a first-class ticket to failure. Simply find a job at an institution where your values are more aligned.

Understand and respect the order. Working towards small changes is fine, but if the order doesn't suit you, either build a new one on your own according to your vision or find somewhere else with an order that better fits your values.

Nature:

Nature is another principle with a double meaning. The first meaning is straight-forward. Make sure you are spending time out in nature, getting sunlight and fresh air. For me, this is one of the reasons golf has become an important hobby. No matter how my round is going on the scorecard, being outside and appreciating all of nature's beauty. It is scientifically proven that natural sunlight is the best way to get Vitamin D (Vitamin D is critical to your immune system and bone strength) and that time in nature decreases cortisol, the stress hormone in the body.

The second meaning is understanding your own and other people's natures. It is similar to emotion, but the key difference here is that emotions are more temporary, whereas nature is more permanent, as in your own and other peoples' personalities. Understanding what motivates people, and what intentions people have.

This aspect of the principle of nature is essentially the key to learning how to play the long game with sustained strategy. This is how you play to win in situations where the circumstances aren't in your favor (newsflash—they rarely are). Understanding your nature and that of other people is how you accumulate power and influence in your career, and always remember, "With great power comes great responsibility."

Attitude:

Attitude is entirely straightforward. It is your mindset, your attitude, your thought processes, and how you choose to perceive life. Guard your mind. Have a powerful attitude in everything you do. I've written extensively on how to develop a strong mindset, so I invite you to reference earlier sections of the book if you need a refresher.

Training:

Training is also straightforward but might be the most underrated and underused principle of them all. Knowing something from a factual basis does nothing for you. It is only through training, which is a committed effort made manifest through consistent application of the principles and exercises will my (or anyone else's, for that matter) system work for you.

I can guarantee my system will result in success, but only if you take the training principle seriously.

Excellence:

Excellence is also straightforward and represents the outcome of the successful implementation of all the principles on a consistent, long-term basis. Aristotle said:

"We are what we repeatedly do. Excellence, therefore, is not an act but a habit."

Over time when you put these principles into practice on a daily basis you will see how your life will transform, and everything you do will be accomplished with excellence. It will become part of your DNA.

Not only is excellence the outcome of the system, but it is also the standard. Raise your standards and you will be successful. If you haven't heard Tony Robbins speak on the importance of raising standards, I strongly encourage you to go find those videos, many of them free on YouTube and give them a listen. Raise the bar for yourself and in all aspects of your life strive for excellence.

Eternal:

I am sure by now you can tell my faith is a strong influence in my life. I wanted to be thoughtful, and careful as to how I expressed my faith because it is important for me to be authentic and there is really no way to separate my faith from my experiences and how I perceive reality.

However, I did not want my book, my system, or the RESONATE principles to come across as exclusive. I do believe in common grace, and I do think everyone, despite their beliefs or walks of life, has unique gifts, talents, and potential that should be shared with the world. I also believe everyone is capable of becoming successful, fulfilling their purpose in life, and learning how to achieve the peak performance state of mind.

Lastly, I think the principles and exercises are beneficial and useful for everyone to use to reach their goals.

With that being said, I do think a commitment to following Jesus is complementary to the principles in this book and opens more doors to finding success, peak performance, purpose, and fulfillment in life.

If you are interested in learning more about becoming a follower of Jesus, please feel free to email me at sean@resonate.vision and I would be happy to tell you more about my personal testimony and help plug you into more resources.

If you feel compelled to become a follower of Jesus and have a relationship with God, I invite you to recite a simple prayer:

Dear Heavenly Father,

Thank you for my life. I confess to you that I am imperfect and no matter what I do I will always fall short of the standard of perfection. Thank you for having grace and mercy on me and for sending your Son, Jesus, the Messiah, to take place on the cross. I believe Jesus died for my sins, and in your mighty power was resurrected to defeat the snares of death and sin.

I invite your Holy Spirit to reside in my heart and am now a new creation. Please give me the strength and guide me as a new believer to resources and people I will need to continue my walk with you.

In Jesus' Name I pray,
Amen.

If you do say that prayer, also, feel free to email me at sean@resonate.vision, so I can help provide you with resources and support you along your walk. Welcome to the Kingdom!

Whether or not you make this decision, I want you to know there is no condemnation in my heart for you. All I offer is an invitation, and I understand if you do not want to accept it.

Lastly, I want to thank you for reading my book and supporting me. I hope my message resonates with you.

THANK YOU FOR READING MY BOOK!

CLAIM YOUR FREE WELCOME CALL

Just to say thanks for buying and reading my book, I would
like to give you a free welcome call with me, no strings attached!

Click this link:

https://calendly.com/seankshahkarami/30min

*I appreciate your interest in my book, and value your feedback as it helps me improve
future versions. I would appreciate it if you could leave your invaluable review on
Amazon.com with your feedback. Thank you!*

Made in the USA
Coppell, TX
04 October 2023

22392851R00056